Meet...

SIDNEY NOLAN

WRITTEN BY YVONNE MES
ILLUSTRATED BY SANDRA ETEROVIĆ

RANDOM HOUSE AUSTRALIA

For my family, near and far, big, small and penguin. YM

For my mother and father. SE

A Random House book
Published by Penguin Random House Australia Pty Ltd
Level 3, 100 Pacific Highway, North Sydney NSW 2060
www.randomhouse.com.au

First published by Random House Australia in 2015

This edition published in 2016

Random House Books is part of the Penguin Random House group of companies whose addresses can be found at global.penguinrandomhouse.com/offices.

National Library of Australia
Cataloguing-in-Publication Entry

Creator: Mes, Yvonne, author
Title: Meet Sidney Nolan/Yvonne Mes; Sandra Eterović, illustrator
ISBN: 978 0 85798 590 3 (pbk)
Series: Meet; 9.
Target Audience: For children.
Subjects: Nolan, Sidney, Sir, 1917–1992
Kelly, Ned, 1855–1880 – Portraits
Painters – Australia – 20th century
Painting, Modern – 20th century – Australia
Other Authors/Contributors: Eterović, Sandra, illustrator
Dewey Number: 759.994

Cover and internal design by Christabella Designs
Printed in China through Asia Pacific Offset Ltd

SIDNEY NOLAN

was one of Australia's most renowned artists.

This is the story of how Sidney came
to create his iconic Ned Kelly paintings.

As a boy, Sidney Nolan would listen to his grandfather's tales of his days as a police officer in the Victorian countryside. Sidney's favourite stories were of the famous bushranger Ned Kelly.

THE
GLENROWAN
HOTEL

Sidney imagined the policemen calling out as they circled the Kelly Gang's hiding place. He pictured Ned Kelly striding away from the burning Glenrowan Hotel. He saw the thick, black armour made from ploughs. He had touched that armour once while on a school trip and felt those fierce eyes flash at him from behind the mask.

When he was a young man, Sidney got a
job in the art department of a hat factory.

The work was dull and uninspiring.
So one day he enrolled in evening classes
at the National Gallery School.

But Sidney's favourite place to go was the reading room in the nearby public library. There he read mountains of books, drank rivers of poetry and soaked up the philosophers. He longed to make art like Picasso, Matisse and other modernist artists from Europe.

The modernists believed that art should express ideas through symbols, colours and shapes. They were of the opinion that as the world changed, art needed to change as well. And Sidney felt the same.

MARX
THE BRITISH ISLES
JOYCE
RILKE
AUDEN

Australia seemed so far away from the art and culture of Europe. With no money to travel there, Sidney stowed away on a ship to London . . . but was caught and sent back.

SUGAR
FLOUR
U.K.

As a desperate last attempt, Sidney visited the lawyer John Reed. He had heard of John's love for modern art, and boldly asked him for money to buy a ticket to London.

John Reed was not willing to pay for Sidney's voyage to Europe, but he admired the young artist's courage and was impressed by his work. He invited Sidney to a dinner that would change everything.

John and Sunday Reed's home, named Heide, turned out to be a haven for artists just like Sidney. Painters, poets, writers and musicians would gather to discuss ideas and share their dreams. They made music or wrote poetry, and Sidney painted.

At last, Sidney had found the place he had longed for.

POEMS

On the other side of the world, World War II had begun. In 1942, Sidney was conscripted into the Australian army and stationed around the small towns of the Wimmera, guarding food supplies.

Still, he found time to paint. How he loved the landscape and the light!

When Sidney lost the tops of two of his fingers in an accident, he met soldiers in hospital who had served on the front lines. After listening to their stories of fighting, injury and death, Sidney decided he would not be sent overseas to fight in the war. However, Corporal Nolan soon got his call.

Sidney ran. He hid away, moving between a friend's studio and Heide. His parents were ashamed and his friends were uncomfortable. Still, Sidney painted on.

His thoughts turned to the stories he had grown up with – of another outlaw like him, a rebel on the run.

He used vivid colours to suggest light and heat. The Australian dirt, scrub and trees appeared as they had never appeared before. The paintings were sometimes moody, the landscape sparse and stark.

In the foreground, Sidney forged a figure like no other: a black square with a slit for eyes, sometimes empty like the armour he had touched so many years ago.

Sidney poured his feelings about war and violence onto the hardboard. He poured the adventures of his youth. He poured his modernist ideas. And he poured his secrets that would forever remain hidden behind Ned Kelly's mask.

V. R.
MURDER
OF
POLICE.
£2,500 REWARD

The time had come for Sidney to leave Heide and set out on his own. He bestowed the Ned Kelly paintings to the Reeds. When they first showed his work in Melbourne, the paintings were ignored or mocked.

When the paintings were exhibited in France, however, they were declared the most important art to come out of Australia and the work of a true poet and painter.

Finally, Australia began to embrace Sidney Nolan and his paintings.

ART

Sidney developed a new and exciting way to paint his country's landscape. His art helped Australia to build a new identity after the struggles of two world wars. He travelled all over the world and painted many magnificent stories, but his best-loved works were those brought to life from the tales he first heard as a boy.

TIMELINE

1917 (22 APRIL): Sidney Nolan is born in Melbourne, Victoria. He is the first of four children.

1922–28: Sidney attends Brighton Road State School. On a school trip, he visits the aquarium where Ned Kelly's armour is on display.

1932: Sidney leaves school at 14 years of age, studies art at Prahran Technical School and has various part-time jobs.

1934–36: Sidney attends evening classes at the National Gallery School.

1938: Sidney begins painting full-time. He meets John and Sunday Reed and visits their home, Heide. Sidney marries Elizabeth Paterson, the grand-niece of landscape painter John Ford Paterson. He becomes a foundation member of the Contemporary Art Society.

1940: Sidney designs decor and costumes for Colonel de Basil's ballet production of *Icare*. This is the first of his involvement with many ballet productions. Sidney has his first solo exhibition at his studio in Melbourne.

1941: After the birth of his daughter Amelda, Sidney separates from Elizabeth and moves in with John and Sunday Reed, with whom he has developed a strong friendship.

1942: Sidney and Elizabeth divorce. Sidney is conscripted into the army as part of the Allied effort in World War II, and is stationed in and around Dimboola in the Wimmera region. He paints and draws landscapes and portraits.

1943: Sidney becomes involved with the Angry Penguins, a modernist movement and journal. He contributes articles and paintings and does design work for Reed & Harris publications.

1944: A controversial edition of the Angry Penguins journal, featuring the Ern Malley hoax, is published with Sidney's *Arabian Tree* on the cover. Sidney tries to get a discharge from the army on medical grounds and goes AWOL in July, changing his name to Robin Murray.

1945: Sidney paints the first of his Ned Kelly paintings. World War II ends. Sidney's brother Raymond drowns mysteriously.

1947: After many years of discord, Sidney moves out of Heide, ending his friendship with the Reeds. He leaves the Ned Kelly paintings in Sunday's possession.

1948: Sidney marries John Reed's sister, Cynthia, and adopts her daughter, Jinx. The Ned Kelly paintings are exhibited for the first time by the Reeds in the Velasquez Gallery in Melbourne. Sidney receives a dishonourable discharge from the army.

1949: Sir Kenneth Clark visits Sidney and offers to support him if he moves to London.

1950: Sidney journeys across Europe. This is the start of many years of travelling all over the world.

1954: Sidney is appointed the Australian Commissioner to the Venice Biennale, where his work is shown alongside William Dobell and Russell Drysdale. He starts the second series of Ned Kelly paintings.

1960: The Queen buys one of Sidney's paintings for the Royal Collection.

1963: Sidney receives an OBE for his services to British art.

1965: Sidney finishes an enormous mural, *Eureka Stockade*, for the foyer of the Reserve Bank of Australia in Melbourne.

1969: Sidney receives the Britannica Australia Award.

1976: Cynthia Nolan dies.

1977: Sidney gifts his Gallipoli series to the Australian War Memorial. Sunday Reed donates the first Ned Kelly series to the National Gallery of Australia.

1978: Sidney marries Mary Perceval, Arthur Boyd's sister.

1981: Sidney is knighted.

1982: The Queen awards Sidney the Order of Merit.

1985: The Sidney Nolan Trust is formed to preserve Sidney's organic farm, near Presteigne in Wales, and to provide cultural opportunities for the region.

1992 (28 NOVEMBER): Sidney Nolan dies at his flat in London. He is buried in Highgate Cemetery.

Also in the *Meet* . . . series

Look out for more *Meet* . . . books coming soon